The
Unshakable
TRUTH®
Journey

GROWTH GUIDES
for Adults

Created

*Experience
Your Unique
Purpose*

JOSH McDOWELL
SEAN McDOWELL

HARVEST HOUSE PUBLISHERS
EUGENE, OREGON

CREATED—EXPERIENCE YOUR UNIQUE PURPOSE
Course 1 of The Unshakable Truth® Journey Growth Guides
Copyright © 2011 by Josh McDowell Ministry and Sean McDowell
Published by Harvest House Publishers
Eugene, Oregon 97402
www.harvesthousepublishers.com

ISBN 978-0-7369-4341-3

Printed in the United States of America

11 12 13 14 15 16 17 18 19 / VP-SK / 10 9 8 7 6 5 4 3 2 1

CONTENTS

About the Authors

Authors Josh and Sean McDowell collaborated with their writer to bring you this Unshakable Truth Journey course. The content is based upon Scripture and the McDowells' book *The Unshakable Truth*.®

Over 45-plus years, **Josh McDowell** has spoken to more than 10 million people in 120 countries about the evidence for Christianity and the difference the Christian faith makes in the world. He has authored or coauthored more than 120 books (with more than 51 million copies in print), including such classics as *More Than a Carpenter* and *New Evidence That Demands a Verdict*.

Sean McDowell is an educator and a popular speaker at schools, churches, and conferences nationwide. He is author of *Ethix: Being Bold in a Whatever World*, coauthor of *Understanding Intelligent Design*, and general editor of *Apologetics for a New Generation* and *The Apologetics Study Bible for Students*. He is currently pursuing a PhD in apologetics and worldview studies. Sean's website, www.seanmcdowell.org, offers his blog, many articles and videos, and much additional curriculum.

About the Writer

Dave Bellis is a ministry consultant focusing on ministry planning and product development. He is a writer, producer, and product developer. He and his wife, Becky, have two grown children and live in northeastern Ohio.

Acknowledgments

We would like to thank the many people who brought creativity and insight to forming this course:

Terri Snead and David Ferguson of Great Commandment Network for their writing insights for the TruthTalk and Truth Encounter sections of this study guide.

Terry Glaspey for his insights and guidance as he helped in the development of the Unshakable Truth Journey concept.

Paul Gossard for his skillful editing of this manuscript.

And finally, the entire team at Harvest House, who graciously endured the process with us.

Josh McDowell
Sean McDowell
Dave Bellis

What Is the Unshakable Truth Journey All About?

You hear people talk about having a personal relationship with God and knowing Christ. But what does that really mean? Sure, they probably are saying they are a Christian and God has personally forgiven them of their sins. But is that all of what being a Christian really is—being a person forgiven by God?

We are here to say that being a follower of Christ is much, much more than that. Everything you are and what you are becoming as a person is wrapped up in it. When Jesus said he was "the way, the truth, and the life" (John 14:6) he was offering us a supernatural way to follow in his way, his truth, and his life. As we do, we begin to understand what we were meant to know and be and how we were meant to live. Actually, when we become a follower of Christ we begin to take on Jesus' view of the world and begin to think like and be motivated like and live like Christ. And that brings incredible joy and satisfaction to life.

So when we see life and relationships as Jesus sees them, we begin to get a clear picture of who we are and discover our true identity. We begin to realize why we are here and recognize our purpose and meaning in life. We begin to know where we are going and experience our destiny and mission in a life larger than ourselves. Being a Christian—a committed follower of Christ—unlocks our identity, purpose, and destiny in life. It is then that the natural process of spiritual reproduction takes place. That is when imparting the faith to our family and others around us becomes a reality. But what is involved in being that kind of a follower of Christ—a person who has joy and satisfaction in life and knows how to effectively impart the faith to the next generation?

The Unshakable Truth Journey gets to the core of what being a true follower of Christ means and what knowing Christ is all about. Together you and your group will begin a journey that will last a lifetime. It is a journey into what you as a follower of Christ are to believe biblically, how you process your beliefs into core values, and how you live them out in all your relationships. In fact, we will take the core truths of Christianity and break them down into a five-step process:

1. ***What truths do you as a Christian believe biblically?***

   In the first step you and your group will interact with what we as Christians believe about God, his Word, and so on.

2. ***Why do you believe those truths?***

   Sure, you can say you believe certain truths because they are biblical, but when you know *why* they are true it grounds you in your faith. Additionally, it gives you confidence to pass them on to others—especially your family.

3. ***How are these truths relevant to life?***

   In many respects truth isn't very meaningful until you see how it is relevant to your own life.

4. ***How do you live these truths out personally?***

   Knowing how the truth of Christianity is relevant is necessary, but what it leads to is understanding how that truth is to become a living reality in your own life. That's where the rubber meets the road, so to speak.

5. ***How do you, as a group, live these truths out before your community and world?***

   As Christians we are all to be "salt" and "light" to

the world around us. In this step you and your group will discover how to impact your own community with truth that is lived out corporately—as a body.

Be warned! The Unshakable Truth Journey isn't a program to study what Christianity is all about. Simply discovering what something is about has great limitations and ends up being of little value. Rather, this journey is about experiencing firsthand how God's truth is to be experienced in your life right now and, in fact, for the rest of your life. It's about knowing God's truth in a real, experiential way. The apostle John said, "It is by our actions that we know we are living in the truth" (1 John 3:19). You will be challenged repeatedly to increasingly know certain truths by experiencing them continually in your relationship with God and with those around you. It is then you will be able to pass on this ever-increasing faith journey to your family and friends.

There will be two specific exercises that appear throughout these courses. The first is entitled "Truth Encounter." This section is an invitation for you to stop and carefully reflect on the truth of each session. You'll be asked to encounter a truth of God as you relate personally with Jesus, as you live out the truth of God's Word with your small group, or as you relate personally with his people. Please don't rush past these Truth Encounters. They are designed to equip you in how to experience truth right in the room you're in!

The second exercise is an assignment for the week, called "TruthTalk." The TruthTalks are designed as conversation starters—ways to engage others in spiritual discussions. They will create opportunities for you to share what you've experienced in this course with others around you. This will help you communicate God's truth with others as you share vulnerably about your own Unshakable Truth Journey.

What you discover here is to last a lifetime and beyond. You will never finish in this life nor in the life to come. God's truths are designed to be enjoyed forever. You see, experiencing God's truth and knowing him will grow throughout eternity, and your love of him will expand to contain it. And that process begins in the here and now. Your relationship with God may have begun 5 months, 5 years, or 50 years ago—it doesn't matter. The truths explored in these courses are to be applied at every level of life. And what is so encouraging is that while these truths are eternally deep they can be embraced and experienced by even a young child. That is the beauty and mystery of God's truth!

This particular Unshakable Truth Journey is one of 12 different growth guides. All the growth guides are based upon Josh and Sean McDowell's book *The Unshakable Truth*™, which is the companion book to this course. The book covers 12 core truths of the Christian faith. The growth guide you have in your hand covers the truth that God *is*—he exists, and he has created us for a reason. Together we will explore who God meant us to be. These five sessions lay the foundation for who we are as God's creation. Check out the other Unshakable Truth Journey courses in the appendix of this book.

Okay then, let our journey begin.

WHAT WE BELIEVE ABOUT GOD

What are your earliest childhood memories about God? Who gave you your concept of God, and what was that concept?

_____

_____

_____

_____

Someone read the following aloud. (This is drawn from chapter 4 of *The Unshakable Truth* book.)

Who is God? What is he really like? We can't see him, and sometimes it may seem he is distant and uninvolved in our world. Yet:

> **We as Christians believe the truth that there is an infinite, personal God of the universe.**

The Bible teaches that a personal being existed before time and space as we know it. This being spoke the words, "Let there be…" and by the power of his will all that exists came into being (Genesis 1:3). We believe those words came from this personal, infinite God who "created everything there is. Nothing exists that he didn't make" (John 1:3). We believe that this God is the Intelligent Designer of all that exists within the universe.

The questions naturally arise, What is the nature of this God? Is he knowable? Why did he create us? While a God with the power to create a vast universe is bound to be beyond our comprehension in many ways, he is knowable to us finite creatures. Although we cannot know him exhaustively, we can know him truly, sufficiently, and with confidence because of *what he has revealed* about himself to us in his Word. There are at least five of his characteristics described in his Word. By exploring them we can begin to know what he is like.

OUR GROUP OBJECTIVE

To gain a greater understanding of what God is like and develop a deeper devotion to him.

||||||||||||||||||||||||||||||||||||||||||||||||||||||||||||||||||||||||||||||||||||||||||

Characteristic #1: God Is Eternal
(He has life without beginning or end)

Did you have a pet when you were young? What is that pet doing now?

_____

_____

Does anyone have a match?—Strike it. How long will it burn? _____ What is the first car you ever drove? Where is it now? _____ Do you remember the first suit or dress you ever purchased? Where is it now? _____

Does everything in your life—material things, natural resources, friends, family, and animals—have an end? As a finite fallen being in a fallen world, everything you experience has an end.

Someone read Isaiah 40:28 and Psalm 102:25-27.

When did God begin? When will he end? _____

_____

Take a moment and discuss together what it means to know a God who is eternal.

|||||||||||||||||||||||||||||||||||||||||||||||||||||||||||||||||||||||||||||||||||||||||||||||||
Suggested questions:

Why would the fires in God's heavenly home never go out? Why would the rivers in his holy city never run dry? Why would the robes he wears never fade or wear out? Why would the people who live with God never grow old? Just what are the ramifications of truly knowing an eternal God?

_____

_____

_____

_____

Isn't our eternal God awesome and really worth knowing? He is worthy of our praise.   /

|||||||||||||||||||||||||||||||||||||||||||||||||||||||||||||||||||||||||||||||||||||||||||||||||
Characteristic #2:
God Is Omnipotent
(He is almighty and all-powerful)

In terms of pounds, how much have you ever lifted at one time? Or in terms of miles, how far have you ever run at one time?

_____

How long can you go without eating? Why do you need to eat day in and day out to gain strength? _____

_____

_____

As finite beings our power and strengths have limits.

Someone read Job 42:2; Psalm 147:5; and Jeremiah 32:17.

Where does God get his power? What sustains him?

_____

_____

Take a moment and discuss together what it means to know a God who is almighty and all-powerful.

||||||||||||||||||||||||||||||||||||||||||||||||||||||||||||||||||||||||||||||||||||||||||||||||||

Suggested questions:

What are God's vitamin deficiencies? When does he tire out? What is the limit to his power? Who can defeat him? Can he accomplish anything he wants? What does it mean to us to tap into God's power and strength for our own life?

_____

_____

_____

_____

Isn't our almighty God awesome and really worth knowing? He is worthy of praise.

||||||||||||||||||||||||||||||||||||||||||||||||||||||||||||||||||||||||||||||||||||||||||||||||

Characteristic #3:
God Is Omnipresent
(He is ever-present)

Someone stand and read this sentence and fill in the blank as appropriate.

"My name is _____. I can see each one of you in this room. I can hear you. I can respond to your voice and your touch. I am now in your presence."

How many places can (the person who read those words) be in at the same time? _____ How many places can his or her presence be known? _____

As finite beings who can be in only one place at a time, think of some of your limitations. You are here in this room with your group without a cell phone and…

- Your child is at school and in five minutes will fall headlong onto a concrete sidewalk. What can't you do? _____

- Your spouse just got unfairly chewed out at work and is sitting in their office discouraged and dejected. What can't you do?

  _____

- You are aware of a vacation package sales scam

that is going around. Your friend is being duped and in two minutes will pay thousands for a worthless vacation package. What can't you do?

_____

- One of your dearest relatives is on the island of Maui. They have just walked down the aisle and right now are having their wedding reception. What can't you do? _____

As finite beings we are limited by time and space.

Someone read Jeremiah 23:23-24; Psalm 139:7-8; and Matthew 28:20.

While it is hard to comprehend, based on these verses, is God with you in the room right now and at the same time with your child who is about to fall, your spouse who is discouraged, your friend who is being swindled, and your relative who is celebrating their wedding? If so, how?

_____

_____

_____

_____

Think a moment and discuss together what it means to know a God who is ever-present.

Suggested questions:

Where is God when you are sleeping and those in Hong Kong are awake? Where is God when you get up and people in Australia are going to sleep? What does it really mean to you that God is always available to you at any time in any place, no matter how urgently others may need him?

_____

_____

_____

_____

_____

_____

Isn't our ever-present God awesome and really worth knowing? He is worthy of praise.

||||||||||||||||||||||||||||||||||||||||||||||||||||||||||||||||||||||||||||||||||||||||||

Characteristic #4:
God Is Omniscient
(He is all-knowing)

Identify a time when you failed a test, forgot the name of someone, made a banking error, or got lost walking or driving a car.

_____

_____

_____

_____

_____

_____

As finite beings we can't know everything.

Someone read Isaiah 46:9-10 and Psalm 139:1.

How much does God know about the past? _____

About the present? _____

About the future? _____

Take a moment and discuss together what it means to know a God who knows everything there is to know about the past, the present, and the future.

||||||||||||||||||||||||||||||||||||||||||||||||||||||||||||||||||||||||||||||||||||||||||

Suggested questions:

Does God have answers for your money problems? Does he have answers for social and racial issues? How about emotional or psychological problems? Does he have answers for relational difficulties? What does it mean to you to have a God who has all the answers to every question and problem that has ever been or will be in your life and everyone else's?

_____

_____

_____

_____

Isn't our all-knowing God awesome and really worth knowing? He is worthy of our praise.

|||||||||||||||||||||||||||||||||||||||||||||||||||||||||||||||||||||||||||||||||||||

Characteristic #5: God Is Personal
(He is relational)

Someone read Genesis 1:26-27.

God said, "Let us" make people. Who is the "us"?

_____

_____

Someone read Genesis 2:18.

What is the remedy for human aloneness? _____

_____

God said to Moses, "You must worship no other gods, but only the LORD, for he is a God who is [jealous] passionate about his relationship with you" (Exodus 34:14).

Why is God such a jealous God? _____

_____

_____

Take a moment and discuss together what it means to know a God who is by nature the perfection of relationship.

Suggested questions:

Why does God want you to talk with him? Why does he want you to get to know him? Why does he want to share with you what he knows? What does it mean to you that the eternal, almighty, ever-present, unchanging, and all-knowing God wants you as his personal friend?

_____

_____

_____

_____

_____

Isn't our relational, personal God awesome and really worth knowing? He is worthy of our praise.

The more we know what God is like and who he is, the more we will want to know him. Our desire and passion to know God is increased as we learn who God really is.

Truth Encounter

Someone read Philippians 3:8.

Imagine for a moment how you would feel if you received a

message that a very special person wanted to meet you. This special someone was powerful and unsurpassed in knowledge, yet was deeply relational and wanted to spend time with you. In fact, this person longed for a friendship with you. How would you feel?

_____

_____

_____

_____

And what if you discovered that this special "someone" was the eternal, almighty, ever-present, and all-knowing God? The incredible truth is that God has given this invitation to you! Someone who is powerful, eternal, unchanging, all-knowing, and deeply relational wants to spend time with you! He longs for an intimate friendship with you!

Reread the apostle Paul's words in Philippians 3:8. He seems to express his own amazement at the privilege of knowing Christ and then responds with a commitment. Paul commits to pursue the surpassing value of deeply knowing Jesus.

Does it move your heart with amazement that the almighty, eternal, ever-present One wants to relate to you? In what way does it amaze you?

Complete the sentences below.

"Lord, as I reflect on the wonder of who you are and yet how you desire to relate to me, my heart is moved with…

_____

_____

_____."

"And I want you to know how I desire to…

_____

_____

_____

_____."

(For example: "My heart is moved with humility and thankfulness. And I want you to know how I desire to know you better. I've been distant from you for too long.")

Take a few moments to share your responses above with your group. Verbalize these sentence prayers so that God might be honored with your openness.

_____

_____

_____

_____

TruthTalk—An Assignment of the Week

God is active and involved with his creation. He entered our world in the form of a human; at the moment of salvation he enters our lives in the form of his Holy Spirit; he answers our prayers and gives us strength through the Holy Spirit, he empowers us to resist temptation and wants to fulfill his purpose in our lives. He is a personal, interactive God who desires a relationship with his creation.

1 "I've been so amazed that an (all-knowing, all-powerful, eternal, and so on) God would want a relationship with me. This truth has been especially meaningful to me this week because…

_____
_____
_____
_____
_____."

2 "I've been learning about some of the characteristics of God in my small group—how he is all-powerful, all-knowing, eternal, ever-present, and personal. I think I need God's presence today. I need the reassurance that he is with me. How about you? What aspect of God's character do you need most today? For example, you might need…

_____
_____

_____
_____
_____."

3 "I like knowing a God who is ever-present. God never abandons us. He is always with us and always acts in ways that show he cares for us. I like knowing a God like that because…

_____

_____

_____

_____."

Read chapters 1 through 4 of *The Unshakable Truth* book as a review of this lesson and chapter 5 for the next session.

‖‖‖

Close in Prayer

How Do We Know God Exists?

Review: How did your TruthTalk assignment go this week? What was the response?

_____

_____

_____

_____

After a few moments of sharing, continue.

Someone read the following. (This is drawn from chapter 5 of *The Unshakable Truth* book.)

> We may *believe* a personal God exists, but can we *know* that he exists? It's not possible to offer absolute proof to someone by having God materialize before him or her and demonstrate his

omnipotence, omnipresence, omniscience, and glory for all to see.

Even if that happened, many people would not accept it as proof. They would wonder if they were hallucinating. In fact, God *did* show up in human form and demonstrated his deity with miracles and prophecies. And people still doubted that he was God.

Yet we are not left without sufficient evidence of God's existence. More than enough convincing data is available for anyone who wants to examine it. God has made himself known to those who want to seek him. Jesus said, "Seek and you will find" (Luke 11:9 NIV). There is evidence of God all around us. His fingerprints can be seen anywhere you look—from the vastness of the universe to the tiniest, submicroscopic cell. Let's look at just three evidences for the existence of God.

OUR GROUP OBJECTIVE

To explore three evidences for God's existence and conduct a role play within the group that equips each of us to share in our own words why we believe God exists.

Evidence #1:
Who Caused All This?

Someone read the following.

Let's walk through a few exercises to help know how to answer a person who might question the existence of God—perhaps even your relative. This is not an exercise to help you "argue" your point—rather, it offers a person information to consider. We will call it "Consider This."

Consider this role play:
"God caused it"

The first role play is a process of logical questions that leads to a reasonable explanation based on a set of natural assumptions. As the person reading this continues, the group should make notes below. The idea is someone in your group will share the essence of this material with another person as a role play exercise.

Here's the information:

Natural Assumptions: 1. All things that begin to exist have a cause of their beginning to exist.

2. The universe began to exist.

3. Therefore, the universe was caused to exist.

4. God by definition is eternal and does not need a cause to exist.

Questions to consider: "What caused the universe and human beings to come into existence?" However a person answers that question you will have a follow-up question: "What caused that?" The logic is that anything that began must have a cause. So you continue to ask, "What caused that?" until there is no answer. Because if God is the uncaused, then logic leads to a natural conclusion: The uncaused caused the known universe and everything in it.

For clarification, someone in your group might want to read aloud page 58 and the top of 59 of *The Unshakable Truth* to the group. Make note below of comments or questions to share at the end of the role play.

_____

_____

_____

_____

_____

_____

_____

_____

_____

Role-play now

[With the above assumptions clearly established, ask the question, "What caused the universe and human beings?" Answers could begin with "Human beings were caused by primates." Then ask, "What caused primates?" Answer could be "Amphibian creatures caused primates." Each answer will eventually take a person to a point of "I don't know what caused X to begin." Your point then is, "Consider the answer 'The uncaused caused it— and that uncaused by definition is God.'"]

||||||||||||||||||||||||||||||||||||||||||||||||||||||||||||||||||||||||||||||||

Evidence #2:
Who Designed All This?

Look at your shoes if they have laces. Look at your watch, your cellular phone, or a clock on the wall. Is it possible that your shoelaces got laced and tied in a bow all by themselves? Did your watch, your phone, or the clock get assembled by chance with no outside help? Why or why not?

_____

_____

_____

_____

A watch, phone, or clock has *specified complexity,* which is the marker of an intelligent designer behind it. The more specified complexity a thing displays, the more it points to an intelligent designer.

Someone read Psalm 19:1-4 and Romans 1:19-20.

It may be quite evident to us that "the heavens tell of the glory of God. The skies display his marvelous craftsmanship" (Psalm 19:1). But to a generation that has been indoctrinated with Darwinian evolution, it isn't always that simple. In today's world, young people are taught by public education that the universe came about by an impersonal force + time + chance. And with enough time, even the most complex beings are possible. But is that really a reasonable explanation?

||||||||||||||||||||||||||||||||||||||||||||||||||||||||||||||||||||||||||||||||||||||||||||||||||||||||||

Consider this role play: "The Intelligent Designer"

Now let's explore how you share with a person in your own words evidence that an Intelligent Designer is behind the universe.

Consider this: A tiny single living cell and the existence of human DNA both cry out for an Intelligent Designer. Have someone read either "What a Single Cell Declares" from *The Unshakable Truth*, pages 60–61, or "Life Requires Vast Amounts of Information" from pages 61–62. You as a group choose which one to focus on.

Then as the person reads, take notes below. The idea is to again prepare to share the essence of that information in your own words in a role-play situation with another person in your group. You are acting as though a friend or relative is questioning the existence of God.

_____

_____

_____

_____

_____

_____

_____

_____

_____

_____

Role-play now

[The question is this: "Did an intelligent almighty God create the universe?" The main point you are making is that the complexity of a human cell or DNA requires too much information or sophistication to occur randomly or by chance. The best and most logical explanation is that a Master Intelligent Designer (God) is behind it all.]

Evidence #3: "I Know Experientially that God Is Real"

Someone read the following drawn from *The Unshakable Truth* book.

A personal experience with God is evidence of his reality. Some might challenge this assertion, saying an experience with God could easily be an illusion or an emotional or psychological fantasy. But those who have genuinely experienced encounters similar to what Paul the apostle experienced on the Damascus road know better. They know it is real. Such experiences are personal affirmations of Paul's statement: "Now that you belong to Christ, you are the true children of Abraham. You are his heirs, and now all the promises God gave to him belong to you" (Galatians 3:29).

It is true that we who are followers of Jesus—children of God—must accept our personal relationship with God by faith. But that doesn't make the relationship any less real. If you have had a personal encounter with the Creator God through Jesus Christ, you know he is real. The evidence of a personal experience with God cannot necessarily be sufficient proof to others, but it can be a convincing argument to the one who knows God personally.

||||||||||||||||||||||||||||||||||||||||||||||||||||||||||||||||||||||||||||||||||||||||||||||

Consider this role play:
"The proof is in the experience"

The question is, "How do you know God exists?" This role play is someone volunteering to share how their firsthand encounter with God made him real to them. Again, this may not be objective evidence of God's existence, but you can encourage a person to experience God through Christ—and they too will know he exists and is real. Make notes below of comments or questions you want to share at the end of the role-play.

_____

_____

_____

_____

_____

_____

_____

_____

_____

Role-play now

Truth Encounter

Someone read Psalm 8:3-5.

Every time you encounter all the things God has created and designed, what are they a reminder of?

_____

_____

_____

_____

There's no doubt that the heavens, the moon and stars, challenge us to explore their cause. It's difficult to study the elements of outer space without asking ourselves how all of those wonders came to be. And the complexities of the moon, the stars, and the solar system are just more evidence of God's creative hand. But of all that God caused to exist, only you and I can relate to him! The moon and stars exist because he spoke them into existence, but they lack the capacity to relate.

The psalmist asked the question, "What is man that you are mindful of him?" His answer reminds us of God's answer: You are the one that God declared is a little lower than the angels. You are the one who is crowned with glory and the honor of relating to the God of creation. You are the one he longs to relate to! You are the priority of his heart and the recipient of his love.

Someone read Psalm 100:1-5.

Based on these verses, who are we and what are we to do?

_____

_____

_____

_____

Complete the sentence below.

"When I consider all that God has created, I am glad that I _____

_____

_____

_____."

(For example: "I am glad that I can share my heart with him. I am grateful that I have sensed his direction in my life and felt his care for me. I am glad we have a God who wants to relate and be a part of our world.")

Now share your expressions of gratitude with your group.

||||||||||||||||||||||||||||||||||||||||||||||||||||||||||||||||||||||||||||||||||
Close in Prayer

Close your time by sharing sentence prayers aloud taken from your expressions of gratitude.

Talk to the Creator and Sustainer of all things. As you do, marvel at the promise that you are ministering to him, bringing him honor and glory as you share your grateful heart.

_____

_____

_____

_____

TruthTalk—An Assignment of the Week

This week take time with a family member or friend and share what you have discovered in this session. Consider saying something like:

1 "When I think about the complexities of _____ (the human body, the solar system, one molecule of DNA, and so on—consider reading from *The Unshakable Truth* book, pages 60–62), I am amazed at God's

The evidence surrounding our universe and life itself simply has too much specified complexity to deny the existence of our Intelligent Designer. That leaves us, as Paul said, "no excuse whatsoever for not knowing God" (Romans 1:20). And in knowing God and reflecting his image we find the joy and happiness he intended… Choosing to believe in God and having a relationship with him gives us a way to understand who we really are.

design. I know God exists because of the amazing way he…

_____

_____

_____

_____

_____."

2 "In my small group we've been discussing the existence of God. Let's say you didn't believe in God. How would you answer these questions?"

- "What caused the universe and humans to come into existence?" _____ (wait for answer and then ask,)

- "What caused that?" _____

- Continue until there is no answer. The uncaused—God—caused the known universe to exist.

3 "I'm so glad we have a God who loves us so much that he gave us so many things in this world to enjoy, like (forests, mountains, planets, animals, and so on). I'm especially glad that God created us to have a special friendship with him. We're the only part of his creation that can be friends with him! I like that because…

_____

_____

_____

_____

_____."

Read chapter 6 of *The Unshakable Truth* book.

YOUR UNIQUE
IDENTITY AS
GOD'S CREATION

Review: How did your TruthTalk assignment go this week? What was the response?

_____

_____

_____

_____

Do people in this group know you for who you really are? Maybe, maybe not. Take a moment to share who you are with those in your group. Sure, your friends may "know" you to a degree, but do you know yourself? Avoid explaining what you do or naming your roles, such as husband, wife, or parent, or nurse or accountant. Instead, describe what makes you uniquely you, your passions, giftedness, personality, and so on. It may be a tougher assignment than you think.

_____

_____

_____

_____

Someone read the following. (This is drawn from chapter 6 of _The Unshakable Truth_ book.)

It is not uncommon for a person to struggle to know who they are and express their identity in clear terms. Somehow, most of us have a slight sense of who we really are as relational beings, but we often need help in discovering the real person, our identity based on who we are, not just what we do.

During the creation process God said, "Let us make people in our image, to be like ourselves. They will be masters over all life…So God created people in his own image; God patterned them after himself; male and female he created them" (Genesis 1:26-27).

God the Trinity—the Father, the Son, and the Holy Spirit—crafted humans in his image. God, therefore, planted deep within us an identifying marker or distinguishing character of his own likeness—the capacity for loving relationships. It is this God-created reality of loving relationships that removes human aloneness and makes you, you. It is

your capacity for relationship that provides all the
meaning, happiness, and joy you could ever hope
to experience.

OUR GROUP OBJECTIVE

To discover a deeper understanding
of who we are and a greater
motivation to explore our full identity
in Christ so we can better serve
him, serve one another, and find a
greater meaning to our own lives.

Based on your knowledge of the relational image of God, what
are some relational traits of God that you have inherited?

Some indication of those traits is found in Genesis 1:1, "God _____
_____." Therefore we all have the trait of _____
_____
_____

In Genesis 6:6, "God _____." Therefore we
all have the capacity to _____
_____

In Genesis 1:4, "God saw that _____."
Therefore we have a sense of _____
when we accomplish things.

In Genesis 6:6, "The Lord was _____."
Therefore we have the capacity to _____

_____

_____

Someone read the following, which continues from chapter 6 of *The Unshakable Truth*.

> God has made you a special, one-of-a-kind person by giving you various **relational talents, spiritual gifts, core values,** and **passions in life**. And he has also placed within you a **distinct personality** that makes you a one-of-a-kind individual—a person designed to do things in ways that only you can do. God has made you in his image like a complex snowflake, a unique person who stands out to him as his special and original creation.
>
> God intends you to use your unique God-given characteristics to relate not only to him but to others as well. "Just as our bodies have many parts," Paul said, "and each part has a special function, so it is with Christ's body. We are all parts of his one body, and each of us has different work to do. And since we are all one body in Christ, we belong to

each other, and each of us needs all the others" (Romans 12:4-5).

There will never be another you. God designed you to fill a role—a purpose—that no one else can fill. You and I want to know our place in this world. God has crafted us specifically for that place that we—and only we—can fill.

The following exercise may be more informative than revealing simply because it is brief. There are at least six characteristics that reflect your identity we mentioned above. Time and space do not allow a comprehensive examination of each. Again, the characteristics that make you, you, are a *distinct personality, talents, spiritual gifts, core values,* and *passions.* We will touch on only two. However, we encourage you individually and as a group to cover these six areas carefully at some point. (We recommend the *Life Keys* book and workbook for adults and *Find Your Fit* book and workbook for young people. We have drawn from those resources here. Check out these books and workbooks at www.LifeKeys.com.)

Know Your Personality

The Myers-Briggs Type Indicator (MBTI) is the most widely used personality test available. The MBTI identifies personality traits in four categories. Getting a feel for the personality traits you possess gives you a clue to how God has placed you in the body of Christ. For "each part has a special function…and each of us has a different work to do" (Romans 12:4-5).

For each set of two selections, check the box that you sense identifies you best. You might get input from others in your group as to whether one trait or the other best reflects you.

❏ I tend to be an extrovert.

Outgoing. You invite others in and socialize. You say what you're thinking and share ideas readily. You have outer energy and tend to take charge of things.

❏ I tend to be an introvert.

Protective. You wait to be invited in and tend to keep to yourself. You keep your thoughts to yourself and share ideas when asked. You have inner energy and tend to step aside and allow others to take charge.

|||||||||||||||||||||||||||||||||||||||||||||||||||||||||||||||||||||||||||||||||||

Sensing vs. intuitive

❏ I tend to be a sensor.

> Practical. You want to know the rules. You strive toward accuracy and a methodical approach to things. You want to stick with something until it's done and use past experience to accomplish it.

❏ I tend to be intuitive.

> Innovative. You want to know the possibilities. You strive toward creativity and a different approach to things. You want to stick with something until you find a better way and use fresh inspiration to accomplish it.

|||||||||||||||||||||||||||||||||||||||||||||||||||||||||||||||||||||||||||||||||||

Thinkers vs. feelers

❏ I tend to be a thinker.

> Logical. You see ideas for data and things. You put business first and set objectives. You are fair but firm—few exceptions. You decide with your head and focus on reasons.

❏ I tend to be a feeler.

> Harmonious. You see ideas for people. You put friendship first and want to know what's meaningful. You are empathetic—make exceptions. You decide with your heart and focus on values.

‖‖‖

Planners vs. perceivers

❏ I tend to be a planner.

> Organized and efficient. You reduce stress by planning ahead. You are systematic and scheduled. You are settled, decided, and make a definite selection.

❏ I tend to be a perceiver.

> Flexible and multitasking. You reduce stress by having options. You are spontaneous and spur-of-the-moment. Open to last-minute information and alternative choices.

Write your personality type here. Share it with your group and tell them why you chose what you did.

_____

_____

_____

_____

_____

_____

_____

_____

_____

Based on who you are personality-wise, explain what type of profession and ministry involvement has best suited you. Discuss this among the members of your group.

_____

_____

_____

_____

_____

_____

Know Your Talents

Your talents usually show up in two or three interest areas of what you like to do.

Tools like the "Strong Interest Inventory" developed by John Holland identify vocational interests and tendencies in people. When a person identifies two or three of these interest areas they gain a deeper insight into how God has wired them. The six interest areas below are drawn from the "Strong Interest Inventory." Check two or three that most apply to you. You might seek the insights of others as you decide which areas reflect you best.

❏ I tend to be a realistic person (R).

> You prefer hands-on activities rather than just reading about things. You like the outdoors and possibly sports of all kinds. You would tend to solve a problem alone rather than work with a group. You would prefer a game of softball over visiting an art museum. You would rather share your ideas than your inner feelings.

❏ I tend to be an inventive person (I).

> You find yourself asking "why" a lot. You probably liked science, math, or chemistry in school. You would rather design your own project than follow the instructions of others. You would rather spend time at a library than at a department

store. Discovering a new idea with a few is more appealing than giving a speech to many.

❏ I tend to be an artistic person (A).

As a kid you probably liked art, crafts, musical instruments, or acting. You like coloring outside the lines. You would rather write a creative story than a report on an existing topic. You would probably rather set your own hours than follow someone else's schedule. You are attracted to the creative and imaginative things of life.

❏ I tend to be a social person (S).

You have natural people skills. You prefer working with a group rather than alone. It's more interesting to plan a party than to balance your checkbook. You would rather make a friend than read a book. People see you as friendly, upbeat, and caring for others.

❏ I tend to be an enterprising person (E).

From the beginning you were a natural-born leader and ready to take charge.

You might have been a schemer as a kid, sweet-talking others into doing what you didn't want to do yourself. You would rather lead than follow and rather give a talk than write a report. You prefer to compete or to argue a point rather than do in-depth research on your own.

❏ I tend to be a conventional person (C).

As a child you probably were a "rule keeper." You tend to search for concrete, black-and-white answers in life as opposed to creative or heavy theoretical answers. You would rather keep score than play in a game or would rather take attendance at than organize a social event. You prefer a methodical life, things that are steady and secure; in fact you may even like to vacation at the same place each year.

Write out the two or three interest areas that best reflect you as a person.

_____

_____

_____

_____

_____

_____

Now share with your group what you have found out. Explore how interest areas equip you with talents to fulfill a special function in life—your vocation, ministry, and work in the body of Christ. Do you see a connection between your personality trait and areas of interest? How?

_____

_____

_____

_____

_____

_____

_____

_____

Someone read the following drawn from chapter 6 of *The Unshakable Truth* book.

> Scripture recognizes our originality. One subtle but powerful indication of this is found in the familiar words penned by King Solomon: "Train up a child in the way he should go, even when he is old he will not depart from it" (Proverbs 22:6 NASB).

Unfortunately, this verse is often misunderstood, and misapplied, by those who are responsible for the training of young people. Some think it means, "Have family devotions, make sure kids attend church and youth group and a Christian school, and then when they are grown up, they will not depart from the faith."

The real emphasis of this verse, however, centers on the phrase "the way he [or she] should go." The writer is referring to the *child's* way, his or her leaning or bent. The root meanings of these words suggest guiding each child according to his or her own uniqueness. In other words, parents must discern exactly who their child is—his or her uniqueness, gifts, interests, and talents—and then draw out and develop that uniqueness. Train the child to be the unique person God relationally created him or her to be.

My (Sean's) parents understood this truth and guided me to understand my "bent"—those talents, gifts, inclinations, passions, and the distinctiveness that made me, me. My dad saw that I had an inclination toward playing basketball. I'm not a tall person; neither is my father. But as a young person Josh excelled at basketball, and he sensed I had the same talent. He encouraged me to pursue it, coaching me as I learned the game. And I eventually fulfilled my dream of being a point guard for Biola University.

My parents also picked up on my inquisitiveness. I wanted to know things; I enjoyed figuring out why this was true or that was true. And I enjoyed sharing what I was learning with others. Because they cultivated my natural inclinations in these directions, I ended up majoring in philosophy and theology and becoming an educator and speaker. All this resulted in my understanding who I am—the unique person God created in his own relational image.

Do you see the importance and value of guiding your own children, grandchildren, and other young people in your life to discover who God designed them to be? What steps can you take to provide that encouragement and guidance?

_____

_____

_____

_____

_____

_____

Other questions you need to consider are these:

• What are the spiritual gifts the Holy Spirit has given you?

- What are your passions in life?
- What are those core values in life that you hold dear?

These are other important aspects of discovering the person called "you."

Discuss the possibility of your group exploring the *Life Keys* course for adults and the youth material called *Find Your Fit* distributed by Life Keys at www.LifeKeys.com.

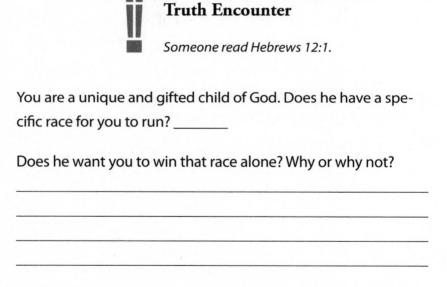

Truth Encounter

Someone read Hebrews 12:1.

You are a unique and gifted child of God. Does he have a specific race for you to run? _____

Does he want you to win that race alone? Why or why not?

_____

_____

_____

_____

We all need the encouragement, support, and challenge of running the race with others. We receive confirmation of "who we are" when we live in community and receive affirmation from our fellow runners.

Now that each person has vulnerably shared about their personality and talents, take turns sharing affirmations of how you or the group has been blessed by each person's unique design.

_____

_____

_____

_____

_____

_____

_____

Consider using a white board or flip chart to list each member's personality and talents. Then verbalize your affirmation of those strengths to one another. Affirm one another by saying,

"_____ (call each person by name), as you described yourself as _____,

I believe our group has been blessed by your _____

because _____

_____."

(For example: <u>Andy,</u> as you described yourself as <u>thoughtful and reflective</u>, I believe our group has been blessed by your <u>careful consideration of your words</u> because <u>you have given great insight during our discussions</u>.)

Celebrate together as each member's uniqueness is recognized.

Close with Prayers

Express your heart of gratitude for God's unique creation—*you!*

TruthTalk—An Assignment of the Week

This week take time with a family member or friend to share what you have learned about yourself and affirm your loved one in their uniqueness. Consider saying something like:

1 "I have a new appreciation and gratitude for the talents and personality that God has given me. I now see how the special way that God has wired me enables me to live out my life purpose by…

_____

_____

_____

_____

_____."

God made us in his image, and when we live out his way, his truth, and his life we find both our true identity and experience pure joy because we are being what we are created to be. We are reflecting his image. Knowing who we are and living as God designed us provide a sense of meaning and purpose to life.

2 "I am so amazed at how God has given you certain talents/personality traits. I can really see how you are learning to use those gifts to live out his purpose by…

_____

_____

_____

_____

_____."

3 "God made only one of you, and I'm so glad that *I* get to be your mom/dad. I can see how he made you special by…

_____

_____

_____

_____

_____."

Additionally, read 1 Corinthians 12:1-12; Romans 12:3-13; and Ephesians 4:11-13. Write out the numerous spiritual gifts found in these verses and seek to know what gifts God has granted you.

Read chapter 7 of *The Unshakable Truth* book.

LIVING OUT
YOUR RELATIONAL
IMAGE OF GOD

Review: How did your TruthTalk assignment go this week? What was the response?

_____

_____

_____

_____

Based on the first four chapters of Genesis, what was the first human crisis? Was it when Adam and Eve sinned, when Cain killed Abel, or what?

_____

_____

_____

_____

Someone read Genesis 2:18.

What crisis did God identify in verse 18, and what was his solution? Also read Genesis 2:24-25.

_____

_____

_____

_____

Notice that this crisis of aloneness occurred before sin entered the Garden. Even in a perfect world, God had a design to remove our human aloneness through an intimate relationship with him and one another.

OUR GROUP OBJECTIVE

To explore and experience
three aspects of relationally
knowing one another, which helps
remove human aloneness.

Someone read the following, which is drawn from chapter 7 of *The Unshakable Truth* book.

> Knowing you are a relational being, created in
> God's image, is important. But how do you live out
> that image in relationship to others? As we stated

earlier, we reflect the image of a relational God in our gifts, talents, values, and so on. These qualities spring directly from the core characteristic that defines God best—love. "God is love," John says, "and all who live in love live in God, and God lives in them. And as we live in God, our love grows more perfect" (1 John 4:16-17). It is as if God wired into us a yearning to live out our relational nature by loving someone and having someone love us deeply enough to explore the depths of who we really are as people created in God's image. And in the process our human aloneness is removed.

The relationships that remove aloneness, those that are lasting and most meaningful, are those in which we come to know another intimately and allow that person to know us equally. That is where the relational love process of knowing and being known comes in.

||||||||||||||||||||||||||||||||||||||||||||||||||||||||||||||||||||||||||||||||||||||||||

The "To Know" Exercise

Someone read Jeremiah 1:5.

God said he "knew" us. The word in Hebrew is *yada,* meaning "to know" in the sense of a deep, intimate acquaintance. God has planted his relational image deep within us, which cries out, "Know me."

Based on last week's session many of you may have come to know each other better. At least two individuals in the group volunteer as those agreeing to "be known." And then the rest of you tell one volunteer at a time what you know about them.

Focus on the positive personality traits and the positive qualities of their interests as you describe what they are like. Feel free to ask them questions to clarify aspects of who they are.

_____

_____

_____

_____

_____

_____

Now you volunteers who were "known" and had your qualities praised, tell the group how that made you feel. And does it give you a sense of deepened relationship with those in your group? Why?

_____

_____

_____

_____

_____

We all want to be known because it removes some of our aloneness. But sometimes we can get the mistaken idea that we have "discovered" the depth of another and there is nothing more to know. Nothing could be further from the truth. It would take a lifetime and beyond to know another person for who they truly are—because we are mysteriously and wonderfully made.

Break into pairs and ask the following simple but revealing questions of each other. See if you discover something you never knew before about that person. Take turns asking three of the questions below and writing down the other person's answers.

- What is your favorite musician or song? Why?

  _____

  _____

  _____

- What is your favorite food? Was that always your favorite food? What is it about that food that makes it your favorite?

  _____

  _____

  _____

- What was your most embarrassing moment in life? I'll keep the story just between us if you want.

  _____

  _____

  _____

- If you could spend a day with anyone from history not living today (other than Jesus) who would that be and why?

  _____

  _____

  _____

- Identify one value or positive lesson your father, or perhaps mother, instilled in you that has special meaning to you today.

  _____

  _____

  _____

After you have taken each other through this exercise, discuss what you might share about your partner with the group that you didn't know before. Then share it.

_____

_____

_____

_____

_____

_____

_____

||||||||||||||||||||||||||||||||||||||||||||||||||||||||||||||||||||||||||||||||||||||||||||||||||

The "To Be Known" Exercise

Someone read Proverbs 3:32.

The word "friendship," "confidence," or "intimate," as it is variously translated, is the Hebrew word *sod*. It means vulnerable or transparent disclosure. The verse is saying God is vulnerable and transparently discloses himself to the righteous. And when we open up to another and reveal a part of ourselves it brings us closer to them—and in the process a little of our aloneness is removed.

Being vulnerable with someone isn't always easy. We sometimes hesitate to do so. Why? What are some reasons we find it hard to self-disclose?

_____

_____

_____

_____

_____

_____

We need to feel safe and know someone will accept us and be understanding when we disclose ourselves.

Break into pairs again and try opening up to each other on a deep level. Take turns asking each other the following questions. Be understanding as your partner becomes transparent.

- Tell me about your dreams, perhaps a hidden dream that has not been realized. What is something you have longed for that hasn't become a reality?

  _____

  _____

  _____

  _____

  _____

  _____

- We all feel happy at times. But what is it that causes you a deep emotional joy—something that touches you profoundly and is especially meaningful to you? It could be something a family member does for you, a place you go, or anything.

  _____

  _____

  _____

  _____

  _____

  _____

- Take your time on this one. Think of a deep-seated fear you have, something you may find difficult to face or talk about, and share it with me. I will listen and be understanding. This too can be kept just between us if you prefer.

_____

_____

_____

_____

_____

_____

After you have taken each other through this exercise, decide whether there is something one of you could comfortably share with the group. If so, share it. Take time for two or three from the group to share their self-disclosure if people are comfortable doing so.

_____

_____

_____

_____

_____

_____

||||||||||||||||||||||||||||||||||||||||||||||||||||||||||||||||||||||||||||||||||||||||

The "Together" Exercise

Someone read Psalm 139:1-3.

The word "know," "acquainted," or "discern," as variously translated, is the Hebrew word *sakan*. It denotes caring involvement.

It is the desire to be involved in another's life—to participate in what they do and be interested in how they feel. It is the idea of "being with" someone through the good times, bad times, and ups and downs of life—always going through it together.

Break into pairs one last time. Ask the questions below of each other, and make a commitment to walk through it together because you want to be caringly involved in each other's life.

- Identify a project or something you have wanted to do for a while that just hasn't gotten done. I want to know how I can be involved with you to help get it done. What would that be?

  _____

  _____

  _____

  _____

  _____

  _____

- Identify a need in your life that has gone unfulfilled. It may be a need I can help meet or something that someone else would have to meet. But I want to be there to help meet it or to pray for you, support you, or comfort you if it is beyond my ability to meet. What is it?

  _____

  _____

_____

_____

_____

_____

Is there anything from this exercise you could comfortably share with the group? If so, share how one of you is going to be "caringly involved" in the other's life.

_____

_____

_____

_____

_____

_____

Truth Encounter

Jesus is our perfect model. He wants us to know him. He has disclosed himself to us in the flesh and in his Word. He invites us to know him for who he is. He knows us intimately and wants to live in us through his Holy Spirit. And he invites us to join him as a caringly involved partner.

Someone read Matthew 11:28-30.

What qualifies you and me to take on his yoke?

_____

_____

_____

What will we gain by being harnessed with Christ as his partner?

_____

_____

_____

Being yoked with Christ, your spouse, and your small group accomplishes many things. And one is this: It reflects the nature of God's image and removes your aloneness.

Yoked with Jesus—A Meditation

Someone read the following.

We all can grow weary in life's stresses. And at times, relationships can be one of our biggest stressors. The people in our lives are sometimes difficult to love and none of us is yet perfect in our ability to love. But there is someone who loves perfectly and his name is Jesus.

Take the next few moments to quietly consider the invitation that Christ extends in the Matthew 11 passage. Meditate on

Jesus. You might imagine him with flowing robes and sandaled feet. In your mind's eye you might see him with a bearded face and nail-pierced hands.

Imagine that Jesus is standing before you in a yoke. He is standing with one side of the yoke around his shoulders while the other side of the yoke stands empty. Listen carefully as you hear Christ's invitation: "Take my yoke upon you. Let me teach you…" The One who IS love can mentor you, teach you, and train you in how to love. The One who knows you, the One who has been vulnerable with you and cares deeply about you, can teach you about relationships, intimacy, and love.

Now carefully reflect on one of your specific relationships that needs more of Christ's abundant love. Could your relationship with your spouse, one of your children, family member, neighbor, co-worker, or a friend benefit from more expressions of your love?

Pause quietly, as you focus on this specific person and imagine Jesus saying, "I am often taking thought of this person, encouraging them, supporting and comforting them, but I often do it without you. Come take the other side of this yoke and together, let's love them well!"

Meditate on this new image of yourself as you stand beside Christ in the yoke. Learn from him. Learn all he knows about loving this person well.

Spend the next few moments in prayer. Verbalize your yielded-ness to the Lord and with your group. Your prayer might sound like:

"Lord Jesus, I look forward to better loving _____ (name a specific person), as I learn from you and partner with you in loving them well."

_____

_____

_____

_____

_____

_____

_____

_____

_____

_____

TruthTalk—An Assignment of the Week

This week share with a family member or friend what you are learning about relationally knowing and being known. Consider saying something like:

Our ethics, morals, social and civic responsibilities, and the capacity to love and be loved come from the fact we were made in God's relational image. We find our true identity in our Creator. And as we live out who we are within the context of God's image and likeness of love, it brings pleasure to him and purpose, meaning, and joy to us.

1 "I've been asking God to help me do a better job of loving others. I've specifically asked him to show me how to show love to _____ by _____ _____ _____ _____ _____ _____."

2 "I've been learning how there are three dimensions to close relationships: getting to know other people, letting them know you, and then becoming intentionally involved in their lives. Which one do you think is an area of strength for me? Which one of these could I grow in? You might tell me, for example, that I need to grow in…

_____
_____
_____
_____
_____."

3 "I would like to get to know more about you and let you know me. What have you always wanted me to know about you? What have you always wanted to ask about me? What could we do together that would be fun—just the two of us? For example, you might have always wanted me to know…

_____

_____

_____

_____

_____."

There is no reading assignment this week unless you are behind on reading chapters 1–7 of *The Unshakable Truth* book.

Close in Prayer

LIVING OUT GOD'S IMAGE BEFORE YOUR COMMUNITY

Review: How did your TruthTalk assignment go this week? What was the response?

_____

_____

_____

_____

Someone read Matthew 5:13-16.

As salt, what are we as members of Christ's body to provide? Being his light, what are we to accomplish?

_____

_____

_____

_____

OUR GROUP OBJECTIVE

To plan a group activity that ministers to a number of people or to our community at large and demonstrates our caring involvement for the sake of others.

Someone read the following.

In this session you as a group are to brainstorm about a project that needs to be accomplished in your community or a need that has gone unfulfilled. This should be something that you as a group can do together as "salt" and "light" to those around you.

Identify a project or something that has needed to be done in your community that you have the power and means to accomplish.

This could be something like mowing the lawn of an elderly couple and weeding the flower beds. It could be helping a single mother who is moving into a different home or apartment. It could be removing graffiti from a bridge or the wall of a building for the city. It could be picking up trash in a community park. This is a project that will let others know you are "caringly involved" in their lives or in the life of the community. Think creatively.

Brainstorm: _____

_____

_____

_____

_____

_____

_____

_____

||||||||||||||||||||||||||||||||||||||||||||||||||||||||||||||||||||||||||||||||||||

Another option:

Identify an unfulfilled need in the life of a person or a group of people. Such involvement could include visiting a nursing home as a group and spending some time just being with and cheering up people who rarely get visitors. It would demonstrate that you care. Or, take a group of disadvantaged children on a trip to the zoo or have a picnic with them as a group. You might work with a local shelter for the homeless or a halfway house and provide a pitch-in meal. You as a group could serve it to them. The idea is to identify emotional, relational, or physical needs that you as a group can help meet in your community.

_____

_____

_____

_____

_____

_____

_____

_____

Take the time here to plan your project using the steps below.

Identify your activity: _____

_____

_____

_____

Set the date and time for your activity: _____

_____

_____

_____

Determine what is needed to execute your activity: _____

_____

_____

_____

Assign responsibilities and tasks. Who will be doing what? _____

_____

_____

_____

Have someone in your group track and record what is being done. This is to record the results of your efforts. _____

_____

_____

_____

Close in Prayer

Bring every aspect of your community activity before the Lord.

Someone read John 13:34-35.

How is living out God's image before your community reflected in these verses?

_____

_____

_____

_____

Assignment of the Week

Execute your activity.

Take the Complete Unshakable Truth® Journey!

The Unshakable Truth Journey gets to the heart of what being a true follower of Christ means and what knowing him is all about. Each five-session course is based one of 12 core truths of the Christian faith presented in Josh and Sean McDowell's book *The Unshakable Truth®*.

The Unshakable Truth Journey is uniquely positioned for today's culture because it 1) highlights how Christianity's beliefs affect relationships, 2) promotes a relational, group context in which Christians can experience the teaching in depth, and 3) shows believers how they can live out Christianity's central truths before their community and world.

More than just a program, The Unshakable Truth Journey is a tool for long-term change and transformation!

CREATED—EXPERIENCE YOUR UNIQUE PURPOSE is devoted to the truth that God is—he exists, and he created human beings for a reason. It lays a foundation for who people are because they're God's creation, who God designed them to be, and how they can live a life of fulfillment.

INSPIRED—EXPERIENCE THE POWER OF GOD'S WORD explores the truth that God has spoken and revealed himself to humanity within the Bible. Further, he gave us his Word for a very clear purpose—to provide for us and protect us.

BROKEN—EXPERIENCE VICTORY OVER SIN examines the truth about humankind's brokenness because of original sin, humankind's ongoing problem with sin, and how instead to make right choices in life.

ACCEPTED—EXPERIENCE GOD'S UNCONDITIONAL LOVE opens up the truth about God's redemption plan. The truth that God became human establishes his unconditional acceptance of us, which defines our worth. God values us in spite of our sin. This is the basis on which we gain a high sense of worth.

SACRIFICE—EXPERIENCE A DEEPER WAY TO LOVE digs into the truth about Christ's atonement. The truth that Christ had to die to purchase our salvation shows the true meaning of love—and how God can bring us into a right relationship with him in spite of our sin.

FORGIVEN—EXPERIENCE THE SURPRISING GRACE OF GOD explores the truth about the power of God's grace. The truth that God can offer us forgiveness in spite of our sin helps us understand how we actually obtain a relationship with him.

GROWING—EXPERIENCE THE DYNAMIC PATH TO TRANSFORMATION speaks to the truth about our transformed life in Christ. The truth about our transformed life in Christ defines who we are in this world and shows how we can know our purpose in life.

RESURRECTED—EXPERIENCE FREEDOM FROM THE FEAR OF DEATH focuses on the truth about Christ's resurrection. The truth that Christ rose from the grave and that his resurrection is a historical event assures us of eternal life and overcomes any fear of dying.

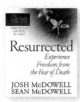

EMPOWERED—EXPERIENCE LIVING IN THE POWER OF THE SPIRIT covers the truth about the Trinity. The truth that God is three in one and defines how relationships work through the Holy Spirit lays the foundation for how we can experience the power of the Spirit.

PERSPECTIVE—EXPERIENCE THE WORLD THROUGH GOD'S EYES examines the truth about God's kingdom and how it defines a biblical worldview. These sessions show how to gain a biblical worldview.

COMMUNITY—EXPERIENCE JESUS ALIVE IN HIS PEOPLE opens up the truth about the church. The truth about Christ's body—the church—provides us with our mission in life and shows us how to experience true community.

RESTORED—EXPERIENCE THE JOY OF YOUR DESTINY is devoted to the truth about the return of Christ. The truth that Jesus is coming back helps us grasp our destiny in life and gain an eternal perspective on life and death.

The Unshakable Truth Journey:
Created Growth Guide Evaluation Form

1. How many on average participated in your group? _____

2. Did you read all or a portion of *The Unshakable Truth* book? _____

3. Did your group leader use visual illustrations during this course? _____

4. *Group leader:* Was your experience connecting to the web and viewing the video illustrations acceptable? Explain.

   _____

   _____

5. On a scale of 1 to 10 (10 being the highest) how would you rate:

   a) the quality and usefulness of the session content? _____
   b) the responsiveness and interaction of those in your group? _____

6. To what degree did this course deepen your practical understanding of the truths it covered?

   ❏ Little   ❏ Somewhat   ❏ Rather considerably

   Please give any comments you feel would be helpful to us.

   _____

   _____

   _____

   _____

Please mail to: Josh McDowell Evaluation
                 PO Box 4126
                 Copley, OH 44321

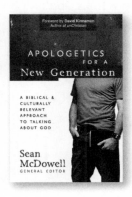

Apologetics for a New Generation
A Biblical and Culturally Relevant Approach to Talking About God
Sean McDowell

This generation's faith is constantly under attack from the secular media, skeptical teachers, and unbelieving peers. You may wonder, *How can I help?*

Working with young adults every day, Sean McDowell understands their situation and shares your concern. His first-rate team of contributors shows how you can help members of the new generation plant their feet firmly on the truth. Find out how you can walk them through the process of…

- formulating a biblical worldview and applying scriptural principles to everyday issues

- articulating their questions and addressing their doubts in a safe environment

- becoming confident in their faith and effective in their witness

The truth never gets old, but people need to hear it in fresh, new ways. Find out how you can effectively share the answers to life's big questions with a new generation.

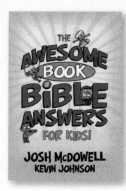

The Awesome Book of Bible Answers for Kids

Josh McDowell and Kevin Johnson

These concise, welcoming answers include key Bible verses and explorations of topics that matter most to kids ages 8 to 12: God's love; right and wrong; Jesus, the Holy Spirit, and God's Word; different beliefs and religions; church, prayer, and sharing faith. Josh and Kevin look at questions like…

- How do I know God wants to be my friend?

- Are parts of the Bible make-believe, or is everything true?

- Was Jesus a wimp?

- Why do some Christians not act like Christians?

- Can God make bad things turn out okay?

The next time a child in your life asks a good question, this practical and engaging volume will give you helpful tips and conversation ideas so you can connect with them and offer straight talk about faith in Jesus. *Includes an easy-to-use learning and conversation guide.*

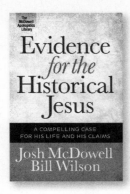

Evidence for the Historical Jesus

A Compelling Case for His Life and His Claims

Josh McDowell and Bill Wilson

After two years of intensive research, the agnostic Josh McDowell was convinced of the reliability of the historical evidence showing that Jesus of Nazareth existed and was precisely who He said He was—God in the flesh. Confronted by the living Lord, Josh accepted the offer of a relationship with Him.

In *Evidence for the Historical Jesus,* Josh teams with writer-researcher Bill Wilson to provide you with a thorough analysis to document that Jesus Christ actually walked on this earth—and that the New Testament accounts are incredibly reliable in describing His life. The authors' broad-ranging investigation examines

- the writings of ancient rabbis, martyrs, and early church leaders

- the evidence of the New Testament text

- historical geography and archaeology

Detailed and incisive but accessible, this volume will help you relate to people who distort or discount Christianity and its Founder. And it will strengthen your confidence in Jesus Christ and in the Scriptures that document His words, His life, and His love.

Why aren't parents the primary disciplers of their children?

Is it even possible to reach today's students and young adults?

Confronting the Fear of Losing Our Kids

Will the majority of our kids continue to walk away from the church and never return?

Involve your church, small group or family in

The Unshakable TRUTH® Journey

To expand the impact of the twelve Unshakable Truth® Journey Growth Guides, a complete collection of teaching outlines, leaders' materials, video clips and powerpoints are available for church, small group and family use. For more information visit:

www.UnshakableTruth.com

"How did the early church effectively pass on their faith to every generation for five generations? We owe it to ourselves and our young people to find out."

Josh McDowell

The Unshakable Truth® church and small group resource collections are part of a unique collaboration between Harvest House Publishers and the Great Commandment Network. The Great Commandment Network is an international network of denominational partners, churches, parachurch ministries and strategic ministry leaders who are committed to the development of ongoing Great Commandment ministries worldwide as they prioritize the powerful simplicity of loving God, loving others and making disciples.

Through accredited trainers, the Great Commandment Network equips churches for ongoing relational ministry utilizing resources from the GC² Experience collection.

The GC² Experience Vision

To provide process-driven resources for a lifelong journey of spiritual formation. Every resource includes intentional opportunities to live out life-changing content within the context of loving God, loving others, and making disciples (Matthew 22:37-40; 28:19-20).

The GC² Experience Process includes:

- Experiential and transformative content. People are relationally transformed when they encounter Jesus, experience his Word, and engage in authentic community.

- Opportunities to move through a journey of…

  - Exploring Truth in the safety of relationship
  - Embracing Truth in a personal way
  - Experiencing Truth in everyday life
  - Expressing Truth through my identity as a Christ-follower

"Most of us have attended too many meetings and have gone through too many courses, only to conclude: We're leaving unchanged, and the people in our lives can see that we're unchanged. It is time to trust God for something different…a movement of life-changing transformation!"

Dr. David Ferguson
The Great Commandment Network

**The Transforming Promise of
Great Commandment/Great Commission Living**
www.GC2experience.com